The Drama of Salvation

What is the Bible all about?
A short Bible Reading Course

John McKay

Kingdom Faith

A teaching sermon on cassette is available to accompany this booklet as part of the short course material.

Copies are available from The Way of the Spirit at Lamplugh House.

First published in Great Britain in 1989 by Kingdom Faith Ministries.

Revised edition 1994

Reprinted in 2000 by The Way of the Spirit
A section of Kingdom Faith Church Trust
Registered Charity No. 278746

Lamplugh House, Thwing,
Driffield, East Yorkshire YO25 3DY.
Tel: 01262 470282. Fax: 01262 470536.
E-mail: info@thewayofthespirit.com
Web site: http://www.thewayofthespirit.com

Copyright © 1989 John McKay.

All rights reserved. No part of this publication may be reproduced, stored in a retrieval system, or transmitted, in any form or by any means, electronic, mechanical, photocopying, recording or otherwise, without the permission, in writing, of The Way of the Spirit.

ISBN 0 9522198 8 3

Scripture taken from the
HOLY BIBLE, NEW INTERNATIONAL VERSION.
Copyright © 1973, 1978, 1984 by
International Bible Society. Used by
permission of Hodder and Stoughton Limited.

How to Use This Booklet

It is arranged in two parts:
- The first (pages 5-19) is a survey-outline of the Bible's story from Genesis to Revelation, told in the form of a five-act play.
- The second (pages 21-26) is a study guide made up of questions that direct your attention to important aspects of the story and their relevance to your own life.

A single teaching cassette with a one-hour talk (sermon) to accompany the study guide is also available. (To obtain this, please write to Kingdom Faith Ministries.)

You can use this booklet in several different ways:
1. By itself with your Bible.
2. Along with the cassette and your Bible.
3. By studying in a group.

Whichever method you adopt, learn to listen for what the Holy Spirit has to tell you—about your beliefs, attitudes and life-style. Ask yourself what lessons you should be learning from your readings, so that you can apply them to your own life as a Christian.

Part Two, the reading guide, has introductory notes on page 17 with further suggestions about how to use it. Each part of this section has questions that will help you determine what you have learned and encourage you to apply that in practical living.

The notes have been prepared in such a way that you can use them privately or in a group. Experience has shown that group study is much more fruitful.

If you use the cassette, you may find it helpful to listen to the relevant part before starting your readings, but if so you should also listen to it again afterwards.

If you use this booklet in a group you will need to listen to the tape early in your meeting. Then discuss your answers to the questions, share your insights and encourage one another to grow in the Lord. Remember to allow time for prayer and fellowship as well.

THE WAY OF THE SPIRIT BIBLE READING COURSE

The purpose of this booklet and the tape that goes with it is partly to give you some impression of how *The Way of the Spirit Bible Reading Course* works. It is not, however, just an excerpt or collection of excerpts from the fuller course, but a properly integrated short course in its own right, and as such is somewhat different in presentation.

- The full course takes you systematically through the whole Bible chapter by chapter with the help of a proper textbook; here you have only a little booklet giving a brief survey of the Bible's story.
- The full course has more comprehensive worksheets.
- The course tapes offer more systematic teaching arranged in twenty-minute parts; the tape accompanying this booklet contains one continuous sermon.

Nevertheless, by using these materials you should capture the flavour of the full course quite well. The purpose of *The Way of the Spirit* is to teach about the livingness of the Bible and the power of the Spirit revealed in its pages, to help Christians understand what the Bible is all about, what the way of God's Spirit is in it, and how to enter more fully into the richness of life men of Bible-times enjoyed. You should find all these aims met in some measure as you enter into *The Drama of Salvation*.

If after this short study you wish to proceed to the fuller course, please write to us for further information, or visit our web site on http://www.thewayofthespirit.com

May God bless you richly as you study his Word.

PART ONE

What is the Bible All About?

Beginning with Moses and all the Prophets, he explained to them what was said in all the Scriptures. (Luke 24:27)

When I was young, like most children, I loved to hear and read stories from the Bible. Certain passages and sentences also became very precious to me. But as I grew older I became more and more puzzled about how these rich gems were held together. What is the overall picture? What is the Bible all about?

I was always fascinated by Luke's record of Jesus' final conversation with his disciples at the end of his Gospel, and just before that with the two on the road to Emmaus, where, 'beginning with Moses and all the Prophets, he explained to them what was said in all the Scriptures concerning himself ... "Everything must be fulfilled that is written about me in the Law of Moses, the Prophets and the Psalms." Then he opened their minds so they could understand the Scriptures.' (Luke 24:27,44f). Jesus clearly taught his disciples what the Bible was all about, and he did not take very long to tell them either, for the journey from Jerusalem to Emmaus was only about seven miles (Luke 24:13).

Of course, we have no record of what Jesus actually said, but here I shall try to do the same kind of thing as he might have done, so that we can see the whole story from Genesis to Revelation, see how it all fits together, and see how Jesus and the Holy Spirit, as well as God the Father, are central to it. In order to do that in a living way, we shall try to follow the story as if we were watching a five act play.

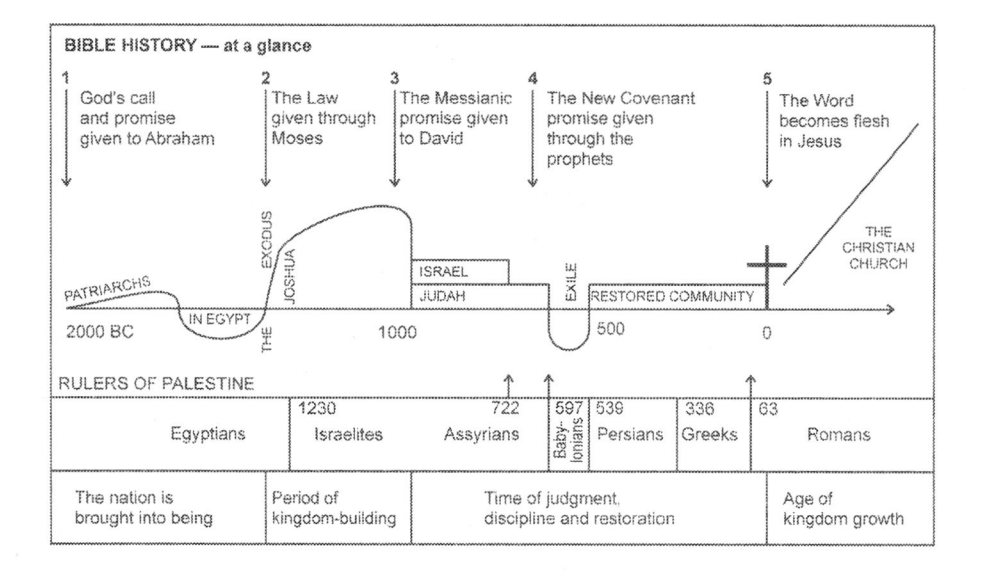

```
BIBLE HISTORY ---- at a glance
1                  2                 3                4                   5
 God's call         The Law           The Messianic    The New Covenant    The Word
 and promise        given through     promise given    promise given       becomes flesh
 given to Abraham   Moses             to David         through the         in Jesus
                                                       prophets
```

                                                                              THE
                                                                              CHRISTIAN
                                                                              CHURCH
                              ISRAEL
 PATRIARCHS   JUDAH   EXILE   RESTORED COMMUNITY
 2000 BC   IN EGYPT   1000   500   0

 RULERS OF PALESTINE

| | 1230 | 722 | 597 | 539 | 336 | 63 |
| Egyptians | Israelites | Assyrians | Babylonians | Persians | Greeks | Romans |

| The nation is brought into being | Period of kingdom-building | Time of judgment, discipline and restoration | Age of kingdom growth |

THE DRAMA OF SALVATION

Imagine you are at the theatre. Before the curtain rises a narrator appears on stage to explain the background to the play you are about to watch. He does so by reciting Gen. 1-11:

PROLOGUE: 'Paradise Lost' (Gen. 1-11)

When God first made the earth, 'he saw that it was good', indeed 'very good' (1:4,10,12,18,21,25,31), and he put man in charge to rule over it. The goodness of his purpose is clearly illustrated in the description of Eden, a place of rustic idyll and harmony, a kind of everyman's Paradise (ch. 2). But man chose other ways than God's and lost it all (ch. 3). Sin, suffering and death multiplied (chs. 4-5), until 'God saw how corrupt the earth had become' and 'his heart was filled with pain' (6:12,6). He showed his judgment by sending the Flood (chs. 6-8), but sin continued to multiply, culminating in the Babel disaster which has resulted in the final alienation of man from both God and his fellow men (11:1-9).

Can God rescue his world? And if so, how? Or will sin continue to thwart his original good purposes? Such are the dramatic questions our play will seek to answer.

> In the Garden of Eden there were two special trees: the tree of the knowledge of good and evil and the tree of life. They represent the twin poles of all God's dealings with men, corresponding to his Word and his Spirit. For tampering with the one, men needed forgiveness, driven from the garden he lost access to the other. Our drama tells the story of God restoring man to a right relationship with both, first through his patriarchs, priests, prophets and kings, then more fully through Jesus, and finally in his New Heaven at the end of time.

ACT 1: God's Covenant with Abraham — His Call and Promise (Gen. 12-50; about 2000-1300 BC)

This first act opens with Abraham on stage being called by God to leave his homeland and co-operate with him in his plan to restore his creation. God promises him four things: a new land, descendants, personal blessing and ultimately blessing through him to all peoples on earth (Gen. 12:1-3). In the rest of Act 1 we watch him and his descendants learning, often through trials and apparent failures, to trust these promises. The essence of God's covenant with Abraham is promise and faith.

Our spirits rise with hope as we watch Abraham leave his homeland and arrive in Canaan (12:4-9), but at the first sign of hardship, when famine strikes, he goes off to Egypt where he ends in a mess and has to be rescued by God and restored to Canaan, where he was supposed to be (12:10 - 13:18). Later in his life we see him head off in the same direction again and with similar consequences (ch. 20), his son Isaac does the same after him, also in time of famine (ch. 26), and finally the twelve sons of Jacob and their families move to Egypt to settle there in very similar circumstances (chs. 42-47).

It was not only the promise of land that proved problematic. Abraham had a terrible struggle for twenty-five years before he came to have proper faith that God would give him a son by his aged wife (Gen. 15:1-6; 16:1-4; 17:17f). His grandson, Jacob, has to go through many years of refinement before he becomes a man of God (chs. 27-35), and Jacob's sons live with strains of jealousy that lead them to the verge of murdering one of their own brothers, Joseph, then selling him for a slave instead (chs. 39f).

While we see evidences of partial fulfilment in the birth of children in Canaan, the final outcome of Act 1 is not exactly a happy one as we watch the promised descendants of Abraham leaving their land of promise and heading off down to Egypt, towards what is eventually to become a life of oppression and slavery.

We cannot but ask: Is God's will to go on being thwarted by man's unfaithfulness? At a purely human level our play already seems to have all the makings of a classic tragedy, the various characters weaving for themselves webs of catastrophe in the face of potentially great happiness.

Yet there is still hope, because our story is not only about men. We have already seen God rescue and restore those he has called more than once and at this point, as the curtain descends, we watch Joseph, now an old man on his death-bed, looking forward in faith, reminding his brothers of the promises God gave Abraham, and assuring them that God will act again on their behalf one day and bring them home (Gen. 50:24).

However, it is now very clear that they need more help from God and that, weakened as they are by sin, they will never make it on their own.

ACT 2: God's Covenant with Moses —
His Word is Revealed
(Exodus - 1 Samuel; about 1300-1000)

Against the background of God's people lost in slavery in a foreign land groaning under their intolerable burdens and crying to God from their bondage, our attention is focused again on one man, Moses. The story of his call introduces a new ray of hope, but the odds against him seem impossible. However, his dogged adherence to God's promise of complete release for the Israelites in the teeth of Pharaoh's increasing hardness against God begins to look like the sort of faith we need to see. The story is full of exciting drama, but the outcome is success. As Moses leads the Israelites out through the Sea and over the wilderness to Sinai, we can at last see how total and unflinching faith in God permits the ready fulfilment of his purposes (Exod. 1-18).

Israel is now free to follow God again, and so, as they enter on the next phase of their history he presents them with a new expression of his will and purpose. His promises to Abraham are now partially fulfilled, but not completely, and they still hold good, but now at Mount Sinai he introduces another covenant. At its heart stand the Ten Commandments (Exod. 20), but it also encompasses almost every aspect of their religious, social and moral life, a total blue-print for their future life as God's holy nation (Exod. 20 - Deut. 26). The heart of its teaching is obedience: Be faithful to God and obey his laws, then you will prosper; disobey him, then you will suffer and perish (cp. Deut. 30:15-20).

The wilderness generation failed to heed the message and because they constantly grumbled and rebelled, they were not permitted to enter the land, but had to wander forty years in the desert (Num. 14; Ps. 95). However, their descendants under Joshua were obedient and successfully occupied Canaan against heavy opposition (Joshua). At the end of his life Joshua reminded them of the need to continue living in faith and obedience (Josh. 23f), but the succeeding generations failed to walk in his ways. They did not complete the work of conquest and even turned to the gods of the Canaanites they should have driven out, with the result that they were repeatedly oppressed by enemies and finally ended up as virtual slaves again, this time to the Philistines who were gaining the control over Canaan that should have been Israel's (Judges - 1 Sam. 13).

The dramatic questions of Act 1 are clearly still with us. To be sure, we now have a nation and it is in its promised land, but the final picture of them hardly inspires great hope that they will ever be a source of blessing to all peoples on earth. They are scarcely a blessing to themselves, let alone others. Sin still has far too strong a hold on them.

However, during these dark years there were a few individuals on whom God's Spirit rested (the judges) and their faith helped to preserve the nation from total extinction. Then in the last moments before the curtain goes down we again see God's Spirit stir among the people, raising up a revivalist prophet, Samuel (1 Sam. 1-3, 7), others to be prophets with him (1 Sam. 10, 19), and finally a king, Saul, who was himself endued with the same prophetic Spirit (1 Sam. 9-11). God has clearly not abandoned his people or his purpose. There is yet hope for better things.

ACT 3: God's Covenant with David —
His Spirit is revealed
(1 Sam. - 2 Kings; about 1000-540)

Many Israelites had thought a king would solve all their problems, but Saul's reign quickly turned sour. After initial signs of promise, we watch his personality progressively disintegrate until in the end he commits suicide after consulting a medium (1 Sam. 13-31). From the start Samuel had warned that obedience to God was the only way to success (1 Sam. 12), but Saul had preferred personal aggrandisement.

The man on centre-stage in this act is David rather than Saul. Just as God had spoken and made covenant with Abraham and Moses, so now he speaks with David after he becomes king, promising that he will be the first of a royal dynasty that will last for ever and through which God will finally bring his purposes to fulfilment (2 Sam. 7). Though David's reign was not without its problems, we do now begin to see evidences of success again as we watch him throw off the Philistine yoke, unite the tribes under his leadership and incorporate the neighbouring kingdoms into a small, but powerful empire (2 Sam.). What he bequeathed to his son Solomon was a kingdom that corresponded in some measure to the vision God had given Abraham and that had recaptured many of the glories of Eden, a land where 'the people of Judah and Israel were as numerous as the sand on the seashore; they ate, they drank and they were happy' (1 Kings 4:20f).

But not for long! Solomon first, and then his successors, repeatedly turned away from the Lord and worshipped other gods. On Solomon's death the kingdom split into two smaller kingdoms, Judah in the south and Israel or Ephraim in the north (1 Kings 1- 13). Despite occasional revivals, the disintegration continued until the Northern Kingdom fell to Assyria in 722 and the Southern to Babylon in 597. The Assyrians virtually wiped Israel off the map of the ancient world, and both they and the Babylonians deported large numbers of the population of both kingdoms to various parts of their empires. The

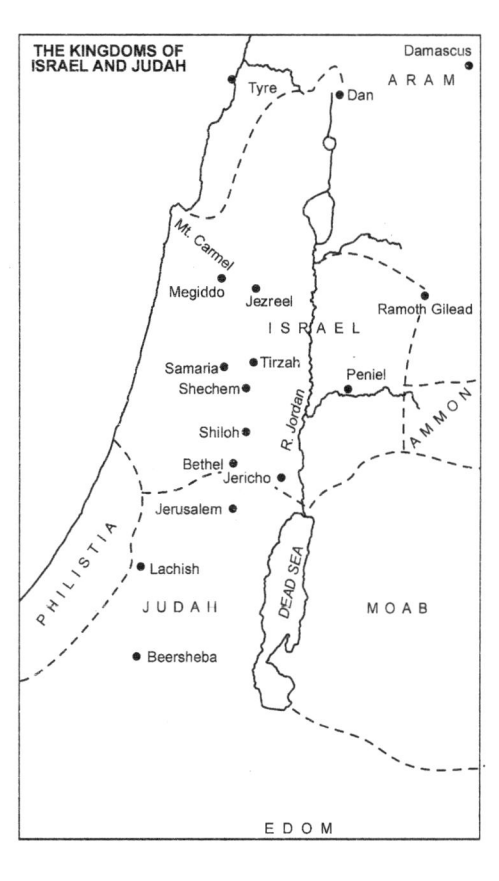

Babylonians eventually destroyed Jerusalem in 587 and so Act 3 ends with the kingdom reduced to a tiny fragment of itself in Judah and God's people mostly scattered abroad in exile, slavery and oppression (1 Kings 14 - 2 Kings 25).

We are left asking the question, as the Jews themselves were (Lamentations): Has God's will finally been brought to nothing? But by now we should have learned to look beneath the stark surface of history and listen for the voices of faith that speak hope for God's purposes.

Beginning in Act 2 and continuing through Act 3 we see a growing movement for revival, led by those we call the prophets, Israel's charismatic enthusiasts on whom God's Spirit rested. Their movement first appeared in Samuel's day. As he led Israel to revival in the eleventh century, he gathered around him a group of like-minded persons who shared in his prophetic endowment (1 Sam. 10, 19). From that time on Israel was never without its prophets, though they were more outspoken at some times than at others. The movement peaked in revival fervour in the ninth century under the leadership of Elijah and Elisha when it found itself locked in a life and death struggle against the pagan forces of Baalism (1 Kings 17 - 2 Kings 9).

From the eighth century on the prophets began to give expression to their visions and hopes in the teachings that have been preserved for us in the books of the great writing prophets. There we hear them calling Israel back to the ancient standards of righteousness and justice (Amos), to knowledge of God and responsiveness to his love (Hosea), to repentance, holiness and faith (Isaiah). In the seventh century the same message was repeated by men like Zephaniah and Jeremiah, and in the sixth by Ezekiel and the 'voice of one calling' in Isa. 40-55.

The main burden of their message is to highlight the terrible dangers of faithlessness and disobedience, just as Moses, Joshua and many others before them had done. They were constantly warning about judgment, suffering and exile, but running through their gloomy preaching is a thread of hope. It is not strongly emphasised by them all, but particularly in Hosea, Isaiah, Jeremiah and Ezekiel we find the growth of a vision that tells of a further act of our play still to come, of a restoration to the homeland and the institution of yet another covenant, but one radically different from the others, 'not like the covenant I made with their forefathers ... because they broke my covenant' (Jer. 31:32). The covenant with Abraham outlined God's programme for salvation, the covenant with Moses outlined the quality of life to be lived by his saved people, the covenant with David outlined his plans for their leader, but this fourth covenant was going to take all these outline plans and promises and make them really work in the hearts and lives of God's people.

First, God will give his people a completely new start by wiping their slate clean: 'I will forgive their wickedness and remember their sins no more' (Jer. 31:34), and second, he will write this new covenant in men's minds and hearts in such a way that they will all 'know the Lord' (Jer. 31:33f) - that is he will take away their sin and give them the will to be faithful. Ezekiel also speaks of this double aspect of the new covenant, but introduces the Spirit as the means whereby God will make it effective: 'I will put my Spirit in you and move you to follow my decrees ...' (Ezek. 36:27).

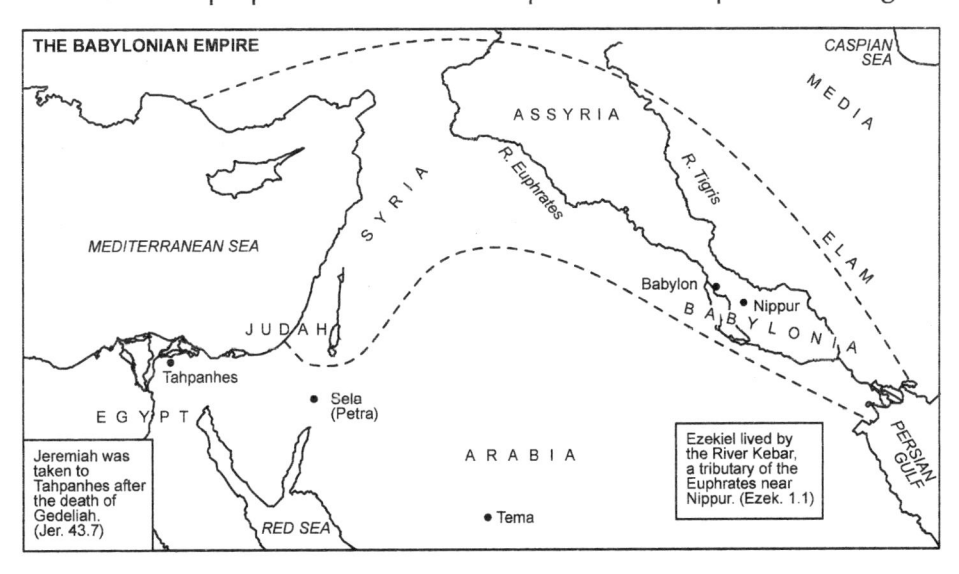

Individual prophets had known the power of the Spirit's working in their lives, but what they now foresaw was a general outpouring of the Spirit in which all men would be able to share in the blessings they had experienced: 'I will pour out my Spirit on your offspring, and my blessing on your descendants' (Isa. 44:3); 'I will pour out my Spirit on all people. Your sons and daughters will prophesy ...' (Joel 2:28).

However, this vision was not exactly new with them, for Moses had glimpsed it on one occasion in the wilderness when God had granted him and his seventy elders something of a foretaste of Pentecost. Then he was heard to say, 'I wish all the Lord's people were prophets and that the Lord would put his Spirit on them!' (Num. 11:24-29). What Moses longed for and the prophets foresaw, the day when all God's people would be prophets/charismatics filled with his Spirit, was in fact the moment when the promise God had made to Abraham to bless all peoples on earth through him would come in great measure to fulfilment.

The prophets also taught that this final act of our play would, like all the earlier acts, be ushered in by one individual who would himself be the first Spirit-bearing man of the new age (Isa. 11:2). In continuity with the covenants of the past, he ('Messiah') would be a descendant of David (Isa. 11:1), through him the righteousness required in the covenant with Moses would be established (Isa. 11:3-5), and according to the promise to Abraham, he would reintroduce the blessings of Eden (Isa. 11:6-9).

Hence we see that much was expected of this coming age, in fact nothing short of radical fulfilment of all God's promises and complete restoration of his initial purposes in creation. However, considering the political progression to this point, it is understandable how those without a prophet's faith would have found such a vision little more than so much enthusiastic froth and bubble offering no substantial basis for hope.

ACT 4: The Close of the Old Age — a Time of Waiting (Ezra, Nehemiah, etc.; 540 - BC/AD)

In 539 the Persians overthrew the Babylonian Empire and many exiled Jews began to return to Israel. A community was re-established around Jerusalem and its initial enthusiasm to rebuild was greatly encouraged by the prophets Haggai and Zechariah, and about a century later by Ezra, the Scribe, and Nehemiah, the Governor.

But there was no real evidence of the ancient promises coming to fulfilment. The voice of prophecy eventually fell silent in the fourth century (Joel & Malachi) and Jewish religion became increasingly legalistic and ritualistic. After the Persians, the Greeks ruled Palestine; then, after a brief spell of independence in the second century the Romans took over in 63 BC.

Again we cannot but wonder whether the great purpose of God had finally come to stagnation. Had it even fizzled out altogether?

The Jews never believed so. At first their prophets maintained them in hope and, when the prophetic voice died, they simply settled down

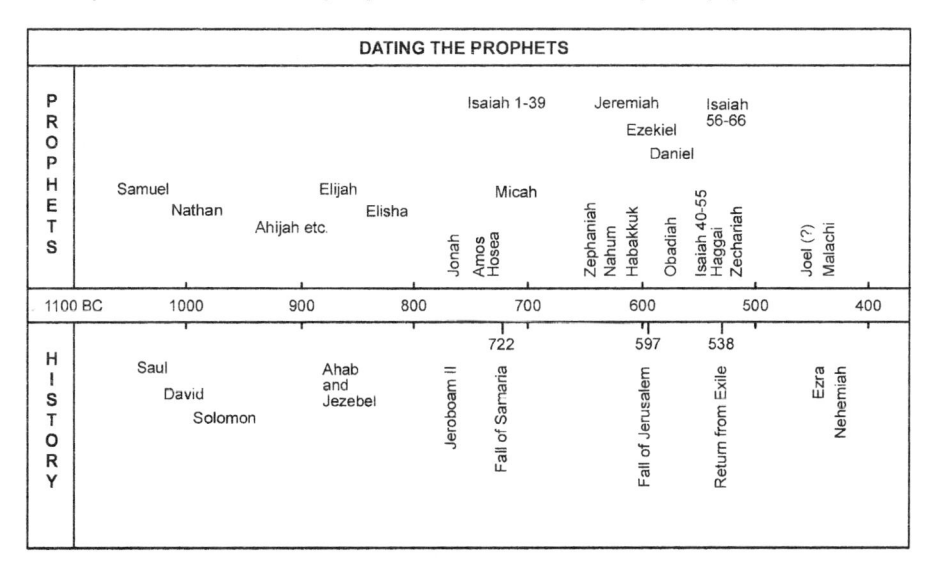

DATING THE PROPHETS

PROPHETS

1100 BC	1000	900	800	700	600	500	400
	Samuel		Elijah		Isaiah 1-39	Jeremiah	Isaiah 56-66
	Nathan		Elisha	Micah	Ezekiel		
		Ahijah etc.			Daniel		
				Jonah	Zephaniah	Isaiah 40-55	Joel (?)
				Amos	Nahum	Haggai	Malachi
				Hosea	Habakkuk	Zechariah	
					Obadiah		

HISTORY

	Saul		Ahab and Jezebel	Jeroboam II			Ezra
	David			Fall of Samaria	Fall of Jerusalem	Return from Exile	Nehemiah
	Solomon			722	597	538	

quietly to wait for Messiah and the new age of the Spirit.

The Exile left waiting Jews strategically placed in all major centres of civilisation. The Greeks gave society an international language and culture. The Romans brought peace to the ancient world and travel became safer than at any time before. By and large the lessons of Moses and the prophets about faithfulness and obedience had been learned by God's people. The time was ripe as never before for Christ to come—all the necessary preparation was completed.

Other significant things had also happened in Israel's history that space does not allow us to examine in depth here. For example, the sacrificial system of worship revealed to Moses and maintained ever since, first in the wilderness tabernacle and then in the temple in Jerusalem, had taught the Jews the meaning of blood- sacrifice for dealing with sin and so prepared them well for the sacrifice of Christ. There was also considerable development in worship (Psalms), and in the appreciation of the wisdom that comes through 'the fear of the Lord' (Job, Proverbs, Ecclesiastes). All of these developments contributed in various ways we cannot pursue here to the development of our drama and the preparation for the coming of Christ.

In fact it is an amazing story we have been following, how God raised up from one man, Abraham, a whole nation of people on the soil of Palestine, and then scattered them through the ancient world so that there were men waiting for Christ everywhere. The course of spiritual preparation is also amazingly precise: first the teaching about the need to relate to God in faith, then about his righteousness (in the Law) and the need for obedience, third about sacrifice for sin through the priestly system, fourth about Messianic hope through the Davidic kings, and fifth about the power of the Spirit through the prophets, all of which prepared the way for Christ's preaching and ministry, his sacrificial death on Calvary and the gift of the Holy Spirit at Pentecost.

ACT 5: The New Covenant —
The Dawn of the Age of the Spirit
(The New Testament; BC/AD -)

Every good play ends with a denouement in the final act, and ours is no exception.

When Jesus appears on stage, he does so amid a flurry of prophetic activity. He is himself born of the Spirit, his birth is announced by angels, and he is recognised by Simeon and Anna who are both mature people of the prophetic Spirit (Luke 1-2). His ministry is heralded by John who comes in the spirit and power of Elijah (Luke 1:17). After 400 years of silence, clearly the prophetic Spirit is stirring on earth once more. Having followed the play as we have, our hopes must surely begin to rise again. Are not these the first stirrings of the dawning of the age of the Spirit we have been waiting for?

As Jesus begins his ministry we cannot but find our hopes being confirmed by all that happens. First we see the Spirit descend on Jesus, and then we watch him enter upon an amazingly powerful charismatic ministry, teaching and performing wonders in the anointing of the Spirit, just like one of the prophets of old, yet with a power and authority hitherto unknown to men. We listen to him describe his ministry in precisely those terms himself when he applies the prophecy of Isa. 61:1-4 to it: 'The Spirit of the Lord is on me, because he has anointed me to preach ...' (Luke 4:18f).

We then see him gather disciples, teach and train them in the gospel work and prepare them for the moment when they will themselves be endued with the Spirit to carry on his ministry after him (Luke 11; John 14-16).

All the dramatic tensions of our earlier acts spring to the fore again as we watch Jesus being betrayed, tried and executed. For one brief moment it seems that it has all come to nothing, but then follows the joy of Easter, and the knowledge of sins forgiven. Then in his last hours with his disciples we see Jesus do the very thing we first mentioned in this booklet, taking them through the whole story again to show them how everything actually hangs together and that the long awaited time of the fulfilling of the Father's New Covenant promise, the moment of the general outpouring of the Spirit that Moses had longed for and that the prophets had foretold, was now at hand. It is little wonder that when he finally was parted from them, they returned to Jerusalem with great joy! (Luke 24:52) These were exciting days. This was the moment all of God's history had been moving towards. The time had come.

After Pentecost, when the disciples were filled with the Spirit and themselves became prophets, or charismatics as we call them today (Acts 2), they carried Jesus' message and his ministry of signs and wonders to the waiting Jews throughout the ancient world. Though many of them refused the gospel, others believed and received the promised Holy Spirit themselves. Many non-Jews also believed and were filled with the Spirit (Acts). The blessing was at last beginning to go out to all peoples on earth, as promised to Abraham. Churches were established all over the ancient world, and though they were not without their problems (we read about some of these in the letters in the New Testament), the early Christians in them found they were living such a life of love, joy and peace that they knew in their hearts that God by his Spirit had granted them a foretaste of Paradise.

EPILOGUE: 'Paradise Regained' (Revelation)

Almost 2,000 years have passed and the hard truth is that Eden has still not been restored. History is littered with evidence of man's continuing unfaithfulness. And, the record of the Christian Church has not always been that good! So we are compelled in all honesty, even at this stage, to raise once more the question that has dogged us throughout our drama: Can God's purpose ever really be fulfilled?

But again we can approach it with hope. At the end of the first century, John, one of Jesus' original disciples, was granted a vision in which he saw down the course of history to come, through many times of trial, to God's final hour, to the blessings of Eden fully restored and man in Christ reigning at the last as he was intended to do at the beginning. In the time that has passed since then the Gospel has indeed reached many peoples and the end John saw is now nearer than most care to imagine. The power of God's Word and his Spirit that worked in creation, that has upheld God's purposes through history, that motivated his prophets, that lived in Christ, that gives us a foretaste of Eden today, still works for the final recreation of all things.

That is our hope! That is our faith!

We have concentrated on the portrait of Jesus as a prophet. Truly he was a prophet, but he was also more than a prophet, for he was 'The Prophet'. In him Word and Spirit come to rest in a unique way, for he alone is 'the Word' incarnate and has 'the Spirit without limit' (John 1:14;3:34). This double aspect of his personality contains within itself the restoration of all that was lost when access to the twin trees of Eden was denied to men. Or, as John the Baptist puts it, he is 'the Lamb of God, who takes away the sin of the world' and also 'he who will baptise with the Holy Spirit' (John 1:29, 33). Jesus' prophetic calling to usher in the New Covenant with its removal of sin and gift of the Spirit is the breakthrough in history that the old covenants looked forward to for setting in motion God's final thrust towards restoring Paradise.

PART TWO

Study Guide

These notes will help you to focus on the central themes of the Bible's story and stimulate further thought for discussion in groups and for personal application in life.

1. First, read the pages above corresponding to the section of notes you are about to use (page references are given in italics).
2. Then look up the Biblical passages they refer to. Some are brief, others refer to whole books or sections of books. With the longer ones flick over the pages of the Bible to get the drift of the story, but read the shorter ones more carefully.
3. Now turn to these notes and look up the set passages, most of which are the same as the ones you will just have read. This time read them with the questions in mind.
4. Write down your answers, as briefly as possible, using only a few words, or at most a couple of sentences each time. As you do so, pray the Lord will show you how your reading and answers are to relate to your own life as a Christian.
5. If you discuss the readings in a group, try to stick to the set themes. It is so easy to go off at tangents, consider many interesting topics, and in the end miss the whole purpose of the study. The questions are to help you avoid doing that, by keeping your thoughts directed to the important, central issues.
6. If you use the tape that goes with this booklet, listen to it straight through in one sitting before you start your study; then listen to it again in parts relating to the study you are doing at the time. It contains one continuous sermon, unlike *The Way of the Spirit Bible Reading Course* tapes that have systematic teaching arranged in twenty-minute parts.

1. God's Covenant with Abraham *(pages 5-8)*

All your questions need to be examined and answered in the light of God's promise in Gen. 12:1-3. Read these verses very carefully. The key words to keep in mind while you read are "promise" and "faith", that is, with respect to God's promise and our need for faith in it.

Gen. 12:1-3

List the things God promised to Abraham.

Gen. 12:4-20; 26:1-11; 46:1-4

How did Abraham and his children handle the promise of land?

Gen. 15:1-6; 16:1-4; 17:17-21

How did Abraham handle the promise of descendants?

Gen. 13:14-17; 17:1-8; 28:10-15; 50:24f

How did God sustain them in his promises?

Genesis Review

What have you learned about the nature of God from reading the Genesis stories?

What have you learned about faith?

How are you going to apply what you have learned in your own walk with God?

How would you summarise the long-term purposes of God as revealed to Abraham?

How much of them do you see fulfilled in Genesis?

What remained to be fulfilled at the end of Genesis?

What remains to be fulfilled today?

What ground its there to hope they will yet be fulfilled?

2. God's Covenant with Moses *(pages 9-10)*

The heart of God's covenant with Moses is probably the best summarised in Exod. 19:4-6. Read these verses carefully and keep them in mind when you answer the questions. The key words this time are "command", "obedience" and "repentance"; referring to God's command or will and the response required of us in obedience, and sometimes repentance.

Exod. 3:16f; 19:4-6

What was God's purpose for Israel?

Exod. 20:1-17; Lev. 18:1-5; 19:2; 20:7f

What is God's standard for his people? How are we to live up to it?

Deut. 30

Are there really only two ways in life? No middle way? How absolute is God's requirement? What hope is there for those who rebel?

Num. 13-14; Ps. 95; Heb. 3:12 - 4:7

What lessons do you learn from this story about moving in faith and obedience?

Josh. 23

How would you sum up Joshua's challenge to Israel? And to yourself?

Judg. 2:6 - 3:6

What went wrong in the period of the judges?

1 Sam. 7:2-6

How did Samuel get revival? What is the gist of his message? Is it still important for us to preach the same message?

3. God's Covenant with David *(pages 10-14)*

This section covers the whole of the books of Samuel and Kings, so skim through some of it to get the story in outline. The key passage this time is in 2 Sam. 7:5-16, particularly vv. 12-16. And note especially the words "for ever", referring to the assuredness of God's promise.

1 Sam. 12

What is required of Israel now it has a king? (See esp. vv. 14f.) What difference does the system of government we have make to what God requires of us today?

2 Sam. 7:1-16

What did God promise to David?

1 Kings 4:20f

How would you interpret the significance of these verses?

1 Kings 11:1-4,23,26-40

What went wrong with Solomon's kingdom?

2 Kings 21:1-16

What continued to be wrong?

2 Chron. 36:11-20

Why did Jerusalem have to be destroyed? Was there no option?

God made huge promises to David about the future of his dynasty and his kingdom. Why were they not fulfilled in the days of the kings?

Isa. 9:2-7; 11:1-9

How do these prophecies relate to God's promise to David?

What relevance for yourself do you see in God's promise to David?

4. Prophets and a New Covenant *(pages 15-16)*

Now we turn to the prophets. The passages to focus attention on are those that tell about the coming New Covenant age, the age of the Spirit: such as Jer. 31:31-34; Ezek. 36:24-32; Joel 2:28-32. The key words this time are "forgive" and "Spirit", referring to the cleansing we receive in Christ and the empowering we receive from the Spirit.

1 Sam. 10:5f,9-13 & 19:18-24

The first prophets of Israel. What similarities do you see between them and Spirit-filled Christians today?

1 Kings 18

What do you see in Elijah's spirit that you know you need for your own fight against paganism?

Amos 5

How would you summarise Amos' message? Should we still preach this way? How does it relate to the teaching of Moses & Joshua?

Jer. 31:31-34

What will be new about life under the new covenant?

Ezek. 36:24-32

What does Ezekiel add to Jeremiah's teaching about the new age?

Num. 11:24-29 & Joel 2:28-32

What will the power of the Spirit enable us to do?

Isa. 11:1-5; 61:1-3

What is the link between Messiah and the Spirit to be?

5. The New Testament *(pages 17-19)*

Now we come to the fulfilment. Keep in mind the main drift of what you have read so far, and watch for links between what Jesus is and does and what we are to be and do. Perhaps the key passage this time is Acts 2 and the key words "the promise of the Father" or "what the Father has promised".

Luke 1-2

What signs do you see here of the new age of the Spirit beginning?

Luke 3:1-22

What has Jesus baptism to do with the Old Testament promises and what has that to do with us?

Luke 11:1-12

How does Jesus tell us here to prepare for the Spirit's coming?

Luke 24:44-53

Why were the apostles so excited?

Acts 1:1-8; 2:1-41

Do you see why the Spirit is called "the promise of the Father"?

Acts 8:14-17; 10:44-48; 19:1-9

Should we too receive the Spirit in the same way?

The purpose of this booklet is to show that the work of the Holy Spirit is an integral part of normal Christian living. The gift of the Spirit is in fact the very thing that Jesus called 'the promise of the Father' or 'what my Father has promised' (Luke 24:49; Acts 1:4). Millions of Christians around the world today are discovering afresh the power of the Holy Spirit to transform their lives and lift them out of the barrenness of religion (or no religion) into the fruitfulness of the life-quality of Eden. You will hear them speak about the surprising reality of what Paul calls 'the fruit of the Spirit': love, joy, peace, etc. (Gal. 5:22). You will also hear them tell of 'power' that has been released in them to bear witness for Jesus (Acts 1:8) and of faith to minister in the way Jesus and the apostles did, with prophecy, healings and other miraculous signs (1 Cor. 12). They will also tell you of new gifts of praise and worship the Lord has put in their hearts, and of the new tongues he has given them to express that praise, just as we read about in the New Testament (Acts 2).

These blessings can be yours today. They are what the Father has promised you, and as we have seen throughout our drama, God is always faithful to his promises. Read Acts 2 and Luke 11:1-13, then do exactly as these passages tell you to do: turn to the Lord, seek this blessing for yourself, ask him for it. Rejoice that his promise is for you, and know that, as God is faithful to that promise, the gift is now yours. Just watch how things begin to change for you in the days ahead.

If you need help to enter into the fullness of this blessing, don't hesitate to seek it from other Christians who understand the things of the Spirit and are living in the good of them.